PRAETORIAN PROJECT

MULTIPLYING THE GOSPEL THROUGH MILITARY CHURCH PLANTING

TED BY **CLINT CLIFTON** WITH THE **PRAETORIAN PROJECT TEAM**

PRAETORIAN PROJECT

MULTIPLYING THE GOSPEL THROUGH MILITARY CHURCH PLANTING

EDITED BY:
CLINT CLIFTON

WRITTEN BY:
THE PRAETORIAN PROJECT TEAM

CONTENTS

INTRODUCTION

United States service members wear dog tags – like the ones on the cover of this short book. I remember getting my first set of dog tags and thinking how cool I was. I wore them everywhere, especially the lake, pool or beach, where people would see them dangling from the simple ball chain. I felt like the bare-chested heroes of epic U.S. military cinema. The dog tags made me more macho and tough.

A few months into my service, my dog tags took on a whole new meaning as I was preparing for my first combat zone deployment. On every packing list I received, specific instructions were given for where the tags were to be worn, what information must be on them and how many extra sets we were to carry. One dog tag was even to be laced into my left boot. Someone else had the courage to ask, "Why are we putting a dog tag in our boot?"

"So, if the rest of your body is too mangled to be recognized, we can identify you by the dog tag in your boot," came the reply. From that day forward I could never forget why we wore dog tags. We wore them in the event of our death on the battlefield. Every day I put them on and every time I laced up my boots (especially the many months in combat zones), I was reminded that I was going to die, and today might be the day. The tags were an ever-present reminder of my own mortality.

Your authors are pastors and church planters – even a wife – who need this reminder as we write this book explaining what we are doing to reach military communities. There is urgency to the call we have on our lives. We have the message of salvation to those who are perishing. We believe the message of the gospel has in it the hope of immortality, and so we seek to see that message spread far and wide.

With that in mind we will try, in these pages, to help you to catch a glimpse of the vision that fuels our work, namely, that Jesus' gospel would spread all over the world as it is caught up in the current of movement that surrounds the United States military.

Our strategy is simple – so simple it's hard even to call it a strategy. We want to see men and women serving in the U.S. military become faithful, committed followers of Christ, and then, as their career moves them around, to organize them to form new congregations in places of need. In short, we are aiming to plant a network of gospel-loving churches near military installations worldwide.

PRAETORIAN PROJECT FAMILY TREE

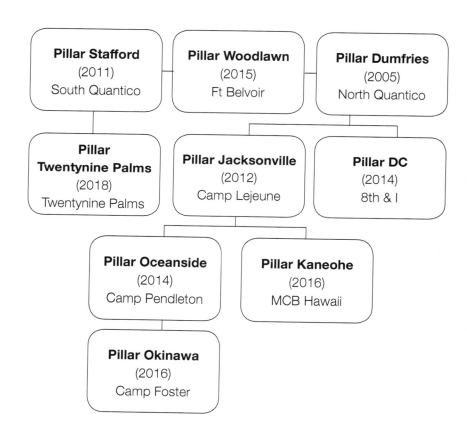

Pillar Stafford
(2011)
South Quantico

Pillar Woodlawn
(2015)
Ft Belvoir

Pillar Dumfries
(2005)
North Quantico

Pillar Twentynine Palms
(2018)
Twentynine Palms

Pillar Jacksonville
(2012)
Camp Lejeune

Pillar DC
(2014)
8th & I

Pillar Oceanside
(2014)
Camp Pendleton

Pillar Kaneohe
(2016)
MCB Hawaii

Pillar Okinawa
(2016)
Camp Foster

1
WHAT IS THE PRAETORIAN PROJECT?

CLINT CLIFTON
PILLAR CHURCH OF DUMFRIES, VIRGINIA

In 2004 God interrupted my life plans by calling me to plant a church near Quantico, Virginia. You've probably heard of Quantico because of one of the half-dozen primetime TV shows set there or because someone you know has been stationed there.

Quantico is nicknamed the "Crossroads of the Marine Corps" because at one point or another most Marines will spend some time in Quantico. Quantico is the combat development command center for the Marine Corps. It is home to the President's helicopter unit "HMX-1," home to the "FBI Academy" and the Marine Corps University, just to name a few.

Every year thousands of service members and their families cycle in and out of Quantico making it both an excellent and awful place to plant a church. Excellent because everyone who comes to Quantico is leaving soon – so the potential for spreading the gospel is unlimited. Awful because everyone who comes to Quantico is leaving soon – so the potential for never really getting established as a church is high.

As God was calling us to plant a church in a place of such transiency, I was confronted with the reality that I knew little about the ins and outs of military life and was clueless about how to reach service members and their families with the gospel. What I did know, which overshadowed my feelings of incompetency, is that I'd been jarred by the words of the apostle Paul in the first chapter of Philippians.

> "Now I want you to know, brethren, that my circumstances have turned out for the greater progress of the gospel, so that my imprisonment in the cause of Christ has become well known throughout the whole praetorian guard and to everyone else."
>
> – Philippians 1:12, NASB

This chapter caused me to wonder if a church could harness the natural movements of Marine Corps (or the military in general) to spread the gospel around the globe? It happened through Paul's witness to the Praetorian Guard; could it happen with my new church and me? These thoughts started to dominate my mind and soon I'd confessed to my wife and my pastor that I thought the best place for us to invest our lives was Quantico.

While I was drawing up my own plans God began to stir me to see the gospel spread through the Marine Corps just as it had throughout the Praetorian Guard centuries before. I know, this was a pretty audacious ambition, but I was too young and inexperienced at the time to realize that. At 24, with a sweet wife and a 3-year-old son, I set out to plant a church near the crossroads of the Marine Corps.

Church planting in Quantico was much more difficult than I anticipated. Secretly I expected that within a year (two at the max) hundreds of jarheads would be worshiping Jesus and hanging on my every word. In reality, I wasn't able to get a Marine to attend a worship service for the first several months. The church was growing slowly but only civilians were participating. I didn't have access to the base and even when I did get around a Marine I couldn't speak his language and didn't know his culture. By year three of this experiment all signs pointed to the fact that my dream would never become a reality and Pillar Church would soon be another casualty on the church planting battlefield.

By God's grace that is not our testimony. Fortunately, great supporting churches and faithful mentors challenged me to press ahead despite my discouragement. Eventually we started seeing modest progress with service members. Some military families joined the church, they invited others and before long more than half of our families units were active or retired military.

Through one-on-one discipleship and preaching I sought to highlight the urgency in multiplication from the Scripture. The net result of this emphasis was men in our congregation expressing an aspiration for gospel ministry. Two of these men were active duty marines with a clear desire to plant churches at other USMC installations (Roy Garza and Brian O'Day, who you will hear from in later chapters). So, after years of discouragement and an emotional abandonment of the praetorian-like gospel movement that first lead me to plant at Quantico, the dream was back on track.

I began teaching these men what I knew about pastoral ministry and providing opportunities in our church for them to gain pastoral experience. Before long, the Marine Corps was pushing these men to move on or transition out. Roy Garza opted to transition out and planted Pillar Church of Stafford on the opposite side of Quantico. Brian O'Day accepted orders to his next duty station (Camp Lejeune, N.C.) with plans to start Pillar Church of Jacksonville as an active-duty Marine. As these men started their new assignments our church did all we could to support them with accountability, mentorship, members and money. Within a year or two both churches were firmly established in their communities and our tiny church planting network was off and running.

The vast majority (some 80%) of Marines are stationed in one of four geographic locations: Washington, D.C., Southern California, Eastern North Carolina and Japan. Consequently, we sought to prioritize the establishment of churches in these locations. To date the following churches are established or are being established:

- Pillar Church of Dumfries (Quantico North)
- Pillar Church of Stafford (Quantico South)
- Pillar Church of Jacksonville (Camp Lejeune)
- Pillar Church of Oceanside (Camp Pendleton)
- Pillar Church of Washington DC (8th&I/Pentagon)
- Pillar Church of Woodlawn (Ft. Belvoir)
- Pillar Church of Kaneohe (MCB Hawaii)

Each of the churches is autonomous – led by local pastors and elders, but networked together for the spread of the gospel. Members of the churches who are in the military are encouraged to view their future assignments as opportunities for kingdom expansion and to strategically request orders to places where new churches are being formed. In many ways, the Praetorian Project is still in its infancy but we have begun to see the benefits of continued discipleship even when geographic locations change.

In my observation, many churches have a positive posture toward ministering to those in the military but few have ever considered that the movements of the military could actually be harnessed for the progress of the gospel. That's what the Praetorian Project is – an effort to multiply the gospel through the establishment of churches near military communities.

2
BIBLICAL RATIONALE FOR MILITARY PLANTING

COLBY GARMAN
PILLAR CHURCH OF DUMFRIES, VIRGINIA

The Praetorian Project was established to strategically apply two biblical patterns to the context of military communities. In this chapter, I want to identify the biblical patterns that undergird the strategy of the Praetorian Project and explain how we are specifically applying these patterns to the context of military communities.

MOVEMENT IS THE METHOD

The first pattern we can observe about the spread of the gospel in the New Testament is that God uses seemingly purposeless (or even contrary) circumstances for the purposeful advance of the gospel. Another way to think about this would be to say, God providentially creates movement that causes the gospel waters to flow to places they would not otherwise go.

One of the earliest examples we could point to is the persecution that arose as a result of Stephen's stoning in Acts 7. Immediately after that event, we read that the Christians in Jerusalem began to scatter. In Acts 8:4 Luke tells us that, "those who were scattered went about preaching the word." From there the text demonstrates that the gospel spread beyond the confines of Jerusalem because of these seemingly contrary circumstances.

The second half of the book of Acts is dominated by one such set of circumstances. When Paul determines to go to Jerusalem it leads to a chaotic chain of events that seem to sideline the world traveler and limit his ability to spread the gospel. Paul's movement becomes limited and provides the perfect contrast for the movement producing activity of God. On the surface, there are attempts at assassination, rigged court proceedings, false accusations and a shipwreck. Not only despite these circumstances, but also through them, God places Paul in a strategic place that he would not have otherwise gone. God places Paul in the most influential city – Rome – among the most influential members of the military, with access to the most influential household. For this reason Paul writes from his cell, "I want you to know, brothers, that what has happened to me has really served to advance the gospel, so that it has become known throughout the whole imperial guard (praetorian in the original Greek) and to all the rest that my imprisonment is for Christ." (Philippians 1:12-13, ESV).

With these examples, we should come to expect that God uses circumstances that cause movement so that the gospel will spread along pathways that we would fail to plan. Military communities are marked by movement that may seem purposeless, but a perceptive church will recognize this movement as purposed by God for the spread of the gospel. As the Praetorian Project has developed, we have worked to harness the natural movements of military life for the spread of the gospel. Many churches in military communities are tempted to grow frustrated with the rate of change and turnover. The result is that the church develops a posture that resists the movement of people that God intends to use for the growth of His body in other places. Rather than resist, we want to resource and challenge the people God has graciously brought into our community so that we send them away with a greater sense of vision and purpose in their next place. By planting churches in as many of the next places they will go, and networking them together for cooperation, it can create a continuity that has often been lacking in the lives of our service members and churches in military communities. The movement is the method.

MULTIPLICATION IS THE MISSION

The second pattern we can observe about the spread of the gospel in the New Testament is that churches are celebrated for their commitment to the multiplication of the gospel in places beyond their immediate scope of ministry and not particularly for their own size. Another way to think about this would be to say that the assignment of every church is the spread of the gospel to places beyond its reach.

Surprisingly, many churches that consider themselves committed to the Great Commission devote little time to seeing new churches established beyond the natural reach of their members. How did we get from "Make disciples of all peoples" to "Share the gospel when and where it is convenient?" We do not hear Paul praising God for how He has used their convenient leftovers to accomplish extraordinary work in other places.

Paul praises the Philippians for their partnership in the advance of the gospel (Philippians 1:5). He praises them for sending Epaphroditus, one of their leaders, to minister with him (Philippians 2:25-30). He even recognizes that their gift and contribution to the work was sacrificial (Philippians 4:18). Churches that understand the Great Commission make sacrifices to put churches (disciple-making factories) in other places so that disciples will be made and the work of the gospel will be extended. In our current climate in North America, there may not be much recognition for a church of 75 people that sends out a church planting team to another community, but the multiplication built into consistent, sacrificial church planting will bear fruit in the long run. Most of the typical commitments to local church growth at the expense of church multiplication are simply short-sighted and out of step with the New Testament.

When you couple a mindset committed to multiplication with the movement of people experienced in military communities it does not take long to realize that military communities offer a unique opportunity for multiplying disciples. The result of biblical cooperation holds the potential to lead to a highly mobilized and motivated group of disciples for the spread of the gospel to the nations.

Understanding these biblical patterns as well as the context of military communities has led us to plant an intentional network of autonomous local churches. Both the network and the autonomy have been important to work effectively toward our goals of multiplying churches in military communities. The network provides the opportunity for long-term investment in individuals as they move throughout their career. The result is that a young Christian may grow in one location, step into leadership in another and prepare for church planting at a third. Over time that provides a consistent crop of church planters and members ready to support the work sacrificially. The autonomy of the local church is critical not only to protect biblical lines of authority and responsibility but also to promote multiplication. It is the calling of the local church to lead the way in church planting. Because of this, our individual churches initiate the church planting work, do the training and work to wrestle out their calling to spread the gospel. The result is a growing number of churches committed to multiplication without the bottleneck created by a heavy centralized structure.

Every context comes with a unique set of circumstances. Many times the challenges are seen as obstacles when God has intended them for gospel advance. If we will be faithful to study the word of God and let it lead our strategies, we will be able to celebrate with Paul when we discover that our circumstances have worked out for the progress of the gospel.

3

THE NEED FOR FAITHFUL CHURCHES NEAR MILITARY BASES

SHAWN BRANSCUM & THOMAS HUDSON
PILLAR CHURCH OF WASHINGTON, D.C.

Faithful churches are needed everywhere, including near military bases. The Praetorian Project aims to plant new churches near military bases because we think military bases are strategic. Strategy, of course, isn't everything so we want to be thoughtful about the type of churches we plant. Obviously, there are churches already established near many military bases. Why does the Praetorian Project make an intentional effort to plant more churches in places where churches already exist? There are two answers to this question.

- **For Continuity in Discipleship.** Our desire is to establish a network of faithful churches that are available for military members as they move locations, from base to base. We're compelled by the idea that a Marine could become a Christian in Washington, D.C., and have a church ready to receive him and continue his discipleship when he receives orders to Southern California. Our network is relatively young, yet we're already seeing the fruit of this pursuit in the lives of Marines and their families that have moved from one duty station to another and been received warmly by a congregation we are closely associated with near another installation. Marines move every two to three years, so it doesn't take long to start to taste the fruit of this effort.

- **For the Spread of the Gospel.** Church planting is about reaching non-Christians for Christ, not simply about providing a church home for the existing Christians in a community. Certainly, every gospel loving church will provide pastoral care, accountability and community for Christians who join, but what about the thousands of families that have no one pursuing them with the gospel? The truth is, in every military community, there are scores of individuals for whom no one is praying or evangelizing. Having more missionary-pastors in a community like this is a benefit to the kingdom of God.

FORM AND FUNCTION

So, what does it mean for a church to be faithful? When we use the phrase, faithful church, we are thinking about both the form and function of a church. Allow me to explain what I mean:

- First, the form is rather simple, in that our network of churches allows us to have a highly vetted group of men who have the same thing in mind when referring to a faithful church. This form, or network, is guarded by us; requiring that our church planters are members of an existing Pillar Church and that their plants ascribe to the same Statement of Faith as the other Pillar Churches. Further, our planters maintain accountability through regular interaction and a commitment to spur one another on to faith and good deeds.

- Second, our function is born out of what the Bible has to say about the Church itself. Matthew 5:13 says, "You are the salt of the earth"; and Matthew 5:14 says, "You are the light of the world, a city set on a hill." Matthew 5:16 says, "Our light shines before others so that they may see our good works and give glory to the father who is in heaven." In other words, the Church exists to display God's glory.

We believe the Church reflects the glory of God to the world when her members are growing, joyful and faithful Christians. This may seem obvious, but at times churches don't do a good job displaying God's character to the world. When members live worldly, self-centered lives, they hide the character of God from the world's view. When churches focus primary attention on fashioning ministries to lure non-Christians into participation without giving consideration to God's design for His Church, the Glory of God that should be beautifully displayed in the church is hidden (Matthew 5:15).

Making the commitment to prioritize spiritual growth can be challenging in this world, where the perception is that God is blessing the churches that are growing quickly. However, we must realize that while sports stadiums, concerts and nightclubs are packed on a regular basis, that does not mean that God is blessing their work. We believe that you can create a buzz or grow a crowd without actually planting a faithful church. Unrealistic and unbiblical expectations can cause pastors and churches to turn to unbridled pragmatism, ignoring or downplaying their responsibility to display God's glory.

In contrast, our churches attempt to guard the image of God through clear biblical preaching, meaningful church membership and a culture of personal discipleship between members. We seek to challenge non-believers to accept Christ and to encourage Christians to grow. However, we do not believe that the responsibility for protecting the image of God falls entirely on the leaders of the church. We believe that it is essential to empower the membership of the church to take on this responsibility as well. One of the most foundational ways we do this is by requiring all potential members to agree to a Statement of Faith before they can become members. As church members understand the weight of guarding the image of God, they are more careful about who they allow into the membership of the church and more intentional to guard one another's lives, making sure they are living in such a way that accurately reflects the glory of God – so that they are obeying the biblical standard. Regardless of how these principles are received, we are committed to the belief that there will be more kingdom impact through the valuing of quality over quantity.

Additionally, we believe the church should act like an assurance of salvation co-op, meaning that if the church is doing their job correctly, the members of the church can be assured, as much as is earthly possible, that they are Christians. They are assured not simply because they have assessed themselves to be Christians, but because others know them and can testify to the evidence of the fruits of salvation in their lives. We work to do all we can to make sure that those who make up our membership are growing and faithful Christians committed together to share the gospel and grow in Christ until His return.

At times, protecting the display of God's image to the world through the church will involve correction. Though not a popular notion in modern churches, Scripture clearly teaches that Christians are to watch one another's lives to protect the Glory of God. If members engage in outward, unrepentant sin, the church should exercise the authority given her by Jesus to call the professing Christian to repentance, following His commands in Matthew 18. Matthew's Gospel tells us that true sheep will ultimately repent of their sin when confronted. Repentance is a sign of spiritual rebirth. Therefore, Christians will repent, giving credibility to their profession of faith. All of this helps prevent confusion from non-Christians regarding the character of God.

With all this in mind, the Praetorian Project intentionally strives to plant a network of faithful churches around the world. We believe that faithful churches will be fruitful churches, unveiling God to sinners through the bride of Christ.

4
PRACTICAL ADVANTAGES TO MILITARY CHURCH PLANTING

JONATHAN RANSOM
PILLAR CHURCH OF OCEANSIDE, CALIFORNIA

I'm going to assume that someone who would venture four chapters into a book about military church planting is potentially considering starting a new church, and is, at least, open to the possibility that this new church would be near a military installation. If that's you, allow me an opportunity to share some of the unique advantages I've noticed, offered in the military context.

MISSION

In the military everyone is evaluated by their mission readiness and capability. This evaluation happens at collective unit and individual levels. Every unit, and every person in that unit, is expected to be ready and able to contribute to the overall mission of the military at any given time. In fact, mission in the military is such a big deal that mission accomplishment actually trumps troop welfare. All that to say this: Mission readiness and mission accomplishment are big deals in the military.

When you plant a church, and seek to make disciples in a military community, you will most likely discover that the people you are working to disciple already speak the language of mission, and, in many cases, are trained and ready to adopt a missional posture, as it relates to living to make Jesus known. As pastors and planters we then have the unique privilege of leading these mission-minded young men and women to see that as noble as their mission in the military may be, and as commendable as their personal sacrifices and contributions towards that mission are, there is a mission that is more noble still. There is a mission that is more deserving of their personal sacrifice. While their mission in the military may contribute to the overall good of people around the globe (Romans 13) there is a mission, in which they can participate, which God has ordained for His glory and for the ultimate and eternal good of people around the globe.

As someone has said, it's not that God's Church has a mission, as much as the mission of God has a Church. When planting churches in a military context you will find a population of people who already speak the language of mission, and in many cases, already know how to adopt a posture of missionally-minded living. They will respond with greater sacrifice and commitment as they learn of God's intent for His Church to be a family on mission – a mission which is more noble and deserves greater sacrifice than any other.

SACRIFICE

The history of our armed forces is replete with poignant examples powerfully illustrating that any mission worth fighting for is almost always accompanied by great personal sacrifice. The history of the Church, and her work to advance the gospel and make disciples over the last 2,000 years is no different. Her mission to know Jesus and make Jesus known moves forward with great personal sacrifice and at great cost. As you plant in mission-minded and mission-postured military communities, you will have the great opportunity to teach with your lips and demonstrate with your lives what it looks like to live on Jesus' mission, for His glory and for the good of people.

You have the privilege of leading young men and women who are already living lives of sacrifice and are ready to respond to an even greater calling, to see what it looks like to pour your life out for Christ. Jesus poured His life out to obey the will of the father and secure our redemption. Paul, and others throughout the New Testament adopted that language and lifestyle, as they too poured their lives out to advance the gospel, to God's glory and for the good of rebels who would be rescued and reconciled to God through that gospel.

As we work to regularly rehearse these truths of the gospel with them, pointing to the great sacrifice at which our salvation was secured, and the ongoing great personal sacrifice of those who have denied themselves, taken up their cross and followed Jesus before us, the privilege is ours to see God awaken the hearts of another generation of young followers of Jesus who will willingly and gladly pour out their lives.

BAND OF BROTHERS

There is something unspeakably powerful about living together on mission. With shared sacrifice, shared suffering and shared pursuit of a mission, comes a relational cohesion and deepening loyalty to each other which simply cannot be reproduced apart from that shared sacrifice and suffering. Again, most young men and women in the military already speak this language and long for this kind of family – this band of brothers. In fact, many young military members come from families with varying and often devastating levels of brokenness and dysfunction, and have turned to the military in hopes of finding this family, which sacrifices, suffers and pursues mission together, and offers deep relational cohesion and loyalty. But, those hopes in most cases are disappointed, and these hurting men and women are left searching for that family to which they can belong.

Here is the beautiful reality. By God's design the Church is not *like* family. His church *is* family. And by His design the Church is meant to be this kind of family. Through the gospel, that family is called to live a life of shared sacrifice, shared suffering and shared pursuit of mission for God's glory and for the good of people. It is a family that offers reconciliation, belonging, loyalty and inseparable bonds – because all of these are deeply rooted in Christ, made possible by Him and sustained through Him. The Church, not the military, is the truest band of brothers (and sisters) and is the family where every wandering and weary rebel can find rest.

MOVEMENT

Military members move a lot. Because of this dynamic, planting a church in a military town is one of the fastest ways to reveal whether your loyalties belong to God's kingdom or to your own. You will labor hard to make disciples of Jesus, but most if not all of these disciples will not remain to help you plant "your" church. Those loyalties will be tested most at the end of your first year when you realize most of your core team has received orders and will be moving, whether they want to or not. And, those loyalties will be tested every month, and every year following. It doesn't end. The turnover rate in military towns, and for church plants in these towns, is constant and can be brutal.

You're left with three options. One, don't plant in a military town. Two, plant in a military town but fight against this cultural reality (not recommend). Three, plant in a military town, fully embrace the constant movement of military members and their families, and leverage that movement as much as you can for the advance of the gospel and the planting of new churches. Think about it. You have the opportunity to pour yourself out training followers of Jesus to know Him and make Him known wherever they live. Then the military will pay all of these people to move to a new community where they can bless another church plant, or join a team working to plant a brand new church.

When you plant in a military community, the defense department is essentially offering to fully fund your missions strategy. Don't fight against it. Rather, embrace this reality for the advance of the gospel, and thank God every day that planting in a military town, with constant population turnover, will keep you humble and completely dependent on His power to build and sustain His Church.

5
EQUIPPING THE SAINTS

BRIAN O'DAY
PILLAR CHURCH OF JACKSONVILLE, NORTH CAROLINA

We plant multiplying churches because we believe this to be the natural pattern of gospel growth outlined in the New Testament. Not only do we get the over-arching idea of multiplication from the pages of the Bible, but we also seek to use the principles the early Church used in multiplication as we equip the saints for multiplication.

THE EXAMPLE – THE CHURCH AT ANTIOCH

"Now there were in the church at Antioch prophets and teachers, Barnabas, Simeon who was called Niger, Lucius of Cyrene, Manaen a lifelong friend of Herod the tetrarch, and Saul. While they were worshiping the Lord and fasting, the Holy Spirit said, 'Set apart for me Barnabas and Saul for the work to which I have called them.' Then after fasting and praying they laid their hands on them and sent them off" (Acts 13:1-3, NKJV).

THE PRINCIPLES

- **First, we function with expectancy.** Notice the church in Antioch hears from the Holy Spirit and acts on it without hesitation or question. It seems that they expected the Lord to continue the work in their midst and beyond. We expect God, as He did in Antioch, to call out men from our congregations to plant. Within our communities of believers, we preach, teach and disciple Christians to always consider the possibility that God may send them out to begin a new church. We talk about church planting; we pray for church plants; we train church planters; we receive updates from church plants; we train people in our midst to be leaders in various aspects of church life – we attempt to live ready for the call.

- **Second, we send out leaders.** In Antioch they had trained up and recognized five leaders that are listed in the text. Then they sent out two of the leaders. Sometimes churches send people out of their churches who are not proven leaders hoping they will be able to start a church. We instead, train and equip leaders in the context of the church and seek to send out those who are equipped and qualified to lead the church.

- **Third, we celebrate subtraction.** The church in Antioch continued their worship of the Lord when the Holy Spirit called out two of the leaders to leave the church and continue the mission elsewhere. We openly rejoice when the Holy Spirit works in a person or group calling them to leave our churches to plant new churches. It is difficult to "lose" people that we love and watch them leave, but we count it as all joy knowing that they are departing to multiply gospel witnesses in other communities.

- **Fourth, we practice church multiplication.** Notice that it is the church in Antioch who is sending these men out. Seminaries and denominational entities are not mentioned. We believe that churches plant churches. This means that we send out church planters from our churches and we only support church planters sent out from other churches. We will not support a church planter who does not have a sending church publically and prayerfully sending him out to plant. If the planter is a member of a church that will not send him out, we will encourage him to join with us for at least a year for equipping and training prior to being ultimately sent out by us. We see seminaries and denominational entities as supporting the work of churches to plant churches and we joyfully work with them in this endeavor.

- **Fifth, we plant in teams.** Just as the church of Antioch sent out Paul and Barnabas together, we prefer to send out two men as planters or, even better, a small team of people who will form the new church.

- **Sixth, we plant multiplying churches.** We train planters to lead their congregations to see multiplication as a natural aspect of a faithful church. The church planter training we use has ten thresholds a church plant must cross to grow into a faithful, autonomous church. The tenth and final threshold is, "Lead Your Church to Plant."[1] Faithful churches multiply.

ONE STORY OF MANY

I was an active-duty Marine and member of Pillar Church of Dumfries when I felt the Holy Spirit were compelling me to plant a church in Jacksonville, N. C. The church celebrated church planting and eagerly anticipated the Holy Spirit sending men out from their midst to plant new churches.

I approached the pastors of the church and told them of the Spirit's prompting in my life. They immediately began to examine me for the biblical qualifications of eldership and train me in pastoring/church planting. Eventually, this church ordained me and commissioned me publically and prayerfully to plant a new church in Jacksonville.

---

[1] This training material is currently entitled "Thresholds" by Clint Clifton. It should be released publically in due time and may be released under a different title.

At their behest, I began to pray for a partner in the work. God provided a partner in Jon Ransom. After Jon and I worked together to plant what is now Pillar Church of Jacksonville and had laid the foundation to include plurality of elders and church membership, Jon felt prompted by the Holy Spirit to plant a new church in Oceanside, Ca. We publically and prayerfully sent him out to plant what is now Pillar Church of Oceanside.

Jon immediately began to pray for a partner in the work. God provided Trace Martinez. They now have a plurality of elders and church membership and are preparing to send out Jon Ransom to plant a church on the island of Okinawa, Japan.

Meanwhile, God provided another man to equip back at Pillar Jacksonville – Johnny Griffith. He was equipped and trained in the context of Pillar Jacksonville and felt prompted to plant a church in Kaneohe, Hawaii. He is currently in Kaneohe and praying for a partner in the work. God seems to be answering that prayer yet again.

This entire timeline is less than five years on a calendar. During the same period, Pillar Dumfries continued planting churches. They planted five churches in these five years and are now a "grand-parent" church expecting to be a "great-grandparent" church sometime next year.

6

CHURCHES AND CHAPLAINS

ROY GARZA
PILLAR CHURCH OF STAFFORD, VIRGINIA

I sometimes get asked the question, "Why are you starting churches at military bases if service members already have chaplains?" The assumption behind that question seems to imply military chaplains can meet the needs of the Christian military community; therefore, it is not necessary to start a church in close proximity to a base. I can understand why this question is asked. I hope to answer that question in what follows.

In 2011, I transitioned out of the Marine Corps to start a new church near Marine Corps Base Quantico. Our desire was (and still is) to reach the Marines stationed at Quantico, the community around us, and any location around the globe that God would lead us. As we started working with the military, there were two pressing issues that we had to resolve as we moved forward – the purpose of the chaplaincy and the purpose of the local church.

THE PURPOSE OF THE CHAPLAINCY

According to a recent military publication on religious matters, the purpose of the chaplaincy is "to accommodate religious needs, to provide religious and pastoral care, and to advise commanders on the complexities of religion with regard to its personnel and mission, as appropriate. As military members, chaplains are uniquely positioned to assist service members, their families, and other authorized personnel with the challenges of military service as advocates of religious, moral and spiritual well being and resiliency."[2]

Life in the military creates a unique situation for the Christian service member. Within the first few years of active duty, a service member will move, on average, three to four times. For the believer, this can be a challenging time in their walk with Christ.

This is where chaplains are a blessing. Chaplains of like-faith can provide chapel services, Bible studies and counseling. Chaplains of a different faith can help facilitate the needs of the service member to accommodate their particular faith group. These services are heightened in a deployment scenario when the service member is far from home and in harm's way. Having a "man of the cloth" on the battlefield provides a sense of comfort to service members, helping to boost morale. Needless to say, chaplains provide invaluable assistance to the Christian service member during times of transition and deployments.

I am very thankful we live in a country that seeks to provide religious services to the members of our military by means of the chaplaincy when a local church is not capable of doing so. Understanding the purpose of the chaplaincy helps make clear that its role is designed to come along side the local church, not to replace the local church.

THE PURPOSE OF THE LOCAL CHURCH

The Church has been and continues to be God's means for advancing the gospel and gathering His people (Matt. 28:19-20). The Great Commis-

---

[2] Joint Publication 1-05. Religious Affairs in Joints Operations. 20 November 2013. http://www.dtic.mil/doctrine/new_pubs/jp1_05.pdf. Accessed September 22, 2015.

sion calls us to make disciples, baptize and teach. This command has been understood as a call to start new churches, not Christian organizations or para-church ministries. Soon after giving this command to the disciples, they spent the rest of their lives starting new churches. The same command is given to us. That's why Jesus said, "Behold I am with you always, to the end of the age." Jesus intends for the Great Commission to be obeyed until He returns. Our commission then, is to start new churches for the advancement of the gospel, the gathering of believers, the instruction of believers and to display God's character to the world.

As we look to Scripture, we see that the 27 books of the New Testament were mainly addressed to churches and church leaders. The Bible assumes that believers are gathered into local assemblies for the purpose of worship, instruction and practicing the ordinances. Not only that, God gifts the Church with leaders and teachers and provides believers with spiritual gifts to be exercised within the context of the local assembly (Eph. 4:11; Rom. 12:3-8; 1 Cor. 12). The Church is encouraged to gather on a regular basis, obey their leaders, commit to one another in such a way that it is clear to each other and the world who is in the Church and who is not, and deal with the sin among those who are committed to our local gathering (Heb. 10:25;13:17; 2 Cor. 2:6; 1 Cor. 5; Matt. 18:15-20).

The Church is God's means of upholding the truth and displaying His manifold wisdom (1 Tim. 3:15; Eph. 3:10). We cannot overlook this fact. While ministries, such as chaplaincy, are a great assistance to the work of the Church, they can never replace the local church. Fortunately, many chaplains understand this and are a blessing to work with.

Planting churches, near military bases or not, is necessary because it's God's means for advancing His gospel and gathering His people. Chaplains provide an invaluable service to military members by facilitating their religious needs until a faithful local church in their area can be established.

When churches and chaplains work together with this goal in mind, the Great Commission is faithfully obeyed and God is glorified.

SEVEN REASONS WHY CHAPLAINCY IS NOT A SUBSTITUTE FOR THE LOCAL CHURCH

Having covered the purposes of chaplaincy and the local church, it may be helpful to hear from a chaplain why chaplaincy must not be viewed as a substitute for the local church. Below are seven practical reasons on this topic from a chaplain in my church actively serving in the National Guard[3]:

1. A chapel service is usually general in nature (as far as Protestants anyway) and usually tries to appeal to as many different Protestant groups as possible.

2. A chapel is a neutral building when it comes to religion and may have many different faiths meeting in it during the week.

3. Chaplains are endorsed to provide religious services and support to military personnel, not to act or function as a church.

4. Tithes and offerings go to the government, not to the "local church." While a local worship service may be able to keep some of it to use for their service, it is still under control of government officials and not the pastor or congregation.

5. There are no offices like elder or deacon, and leaders of the specific chapel service may not necessarily be chosen because they meet the biblical requirements to be an elder or deacon.

6. There is no "membership" and no real ability to do church discipline. Rather discipline is more likely to be military discipline.

---

[3] Chaplain Darren King, LTC. Army National Guard. Email Correspondence. Received September 22, 2015.

7. Chaplains lead specific types of worship services, like the "Baptist Service." When chaplains are on leave, a chaplain of a different faith or theological background may lead that service.

HOW CHURCHES AND CHAPLAINS WORK TOGETHER FOR GOD'S GLORY

Now that we have established the purpose of chaplaincy and the local church, and reasons why one should not take the place of the other, it's important know how we can work together for the purpose of advancing the gospel and bringing glory to God. There are three helpful concepts to consider when working with military chaplains.

- **Person of Peace.** This term is often used on the mission field and according to one mission entity's website, is described: "God often uses a local person to introduce Christian workers into an otherwise hostile community and create openness toward the gospel message. As a result, churches are being planted by the hundreds in places where the gospel had never been preached before."[4] Church planters should view chaplains as a person of peace. They have connections with the military community that you simply won't have. As a veteran Marine, I found it difficult to maintain the type of connection I once had with the military community as an active-duty service member. The chaplain is your connection to military life on base. He is your person of peace.

- **Prayer.** At the beginning our church planting journey, I couldn't even get one chaplain on base to work with me. We had no choice but to pray and leave it in God's hands. God answered our prayers. We began to receive opportunities on base that we didn't even know

---

[4] Erich Bridges. *In Brief, Friend of the Gospel: The 'Man of Peace'.* http://imb.org/updates/storyview.aspx?StoryID=537#.VgQvIVzWobQ. Accessed September 22, 2015.

were possible; from speaking at "welcome aboard" briefs, from movie nights, to sports camps. We haven't stopped praying, and we are continuing to see God at work in ways we could have never imagined. It's important to remember that nothing of great significance will happen without prayer.

- **Patience.** Don't give up. Church planting is difficult. Church planting in a military context is even more difficult. The people you're trying to reach are constantly moving. Not only that, your person of peace, the chaplain, also moves on a regular basis. You have your work cut out for you. As mentioned above, it took time for doors to open for us. Unfortunately, there were times when I tried to force open those doors too soon. Before our first Easter service, with invite cards en masse, several boxes of ready to serve coffee and a zealous volunteer team, we stormed the base, setup shop near the base convenient store, and started handing out free coffee and invite cards to Marines passing by. The only problem was … I didn't have permission to do any of that! We were eventually asked to leave. Not a good way to start your relationship with the base! The military is a disciplined environment filled with rules and procedures. Your only hope of doing any kind of work on base is through the chaplain. With this in mind there are two opportunities you must wait for with patience. First, for a chaplain who is outward focused – meaning he wants to reach people. Second, you need this same chaplain to take you seriously and know that you mean business. This means you must have a game plan. Think about how will you serve the base. Will it be a Bible study, seminar, counseling or an outreach event? We started doing outreach events. We hosted movie nights in the base housing communities and we conducted sports camps for military families. When the base begins to take notice, more doors will open up for you. Be patient. These relationships take years to develop. Don't give up because the results are worth the wait.

The chaplain can be a great partner in the gospel to a church planter. When the purpose of the both chaplaincy and the local church are understood by the planter, he will accomplish his calling with a greater sense of clarity and conviction. He will seek out partnerships with chaplains and view them as person of peace who can create avenues for the work of the gospel to increase on the base. However, he must wait prayerfully and patiently as the Lord moves to open doors.

7
PLANNING AND PROVIDENCE

BRIAN COLLISON
PILLAR CHURCH OF WOODLAWN, VIRGINIA

After 10 years on active duty in the Army as a felony criminal investigator, I responded to God's call to full-time ministry and went to seminary to prepare. I immediately pursued an M.Div. in biblical counseling at Southeastern Baptist Theological Seminary in Wake Forest, N.C.; volunteered in various capacities in a local church; and served in the U.S. Army reserves. I thought I had it all planned out: finish my degree, find a job on staff at a megachurch as a biblical counselor, teach a few Sunday School classes, coach little league. That sounded okay to me. Church planting was not even on my radar. But "Uncle Sam" had other plans.

In May of 2013, I was mobilized with the Army Reserves to serve for a year at Fort Belvoir, Va. This was an unaccompanied tour, so my family remained in North Carolina. I hoped I would find a church where I could be discipled and have opportunities to disciple others. My expectation was that I would serve at Ft. Belvoir and return to my plan in Wake Forest. I got way more than I expected.

God was using this mobilization to place me exactly where He wanted me. At Pillar Church of Dumfries, I was discipled by men who recognized unique gifts and abilities in me that were well suited for church planting. I was challenged to use those attributes to serve God through church planting. My vision of the future of ministry began to change and come into alignment with God's plan: a church plant at Ft. Belvoir.

Through much prayer and conversation with my family, I agreed to a one-year church planting apprenticeship. During this time the gifting of a church building (right outside Ft. Belvoir), the moving of new families, the changing of orders (and hearts), and much inspired sacrifice in so many who have come to serve alongside my family and I, have shown me that God was working all along the way. God can use things like Army mobilization and PCS orders to accomplish His plan, which is so much greater than my own. I now find myself serving alongside a diverse team of military, veterans and civilians to see Pillar Church of Woodlawn begin to take shape. My best strategizing could have never compiled the group that God has placed alongside me.

One of the biggest challenges faced by planters who seek to serve military communities is the transient nature of those communities. Military men and women are expected to move regularly, so most established churches have a difficult time ministering effectively to this population. Many churches do not even attempt to reach the military community for this reason. This is where Pillar Church is set apart.

At Pillar we seek to leverage this transient community for opportunities to spread of gospel. As PCS orders arrive, tension usually builds among military families. The list of unknowns begins to form as the service member prepares for a new assignment, new leadership and a new living situation. But when seen through the lens of the gospel, life on "mission" has a whole new meaning. With new assignments come new gospel opportunities. With new leadership comes new influence. With a new living situation come new neighbors with whom to share the gospel. We know that each moving season brings new opportunities for ministry as God brings new people into our circle of influence.

In addition, we seek to equip this transient community for the spread of the gospel. We know that those who are members here will soon be moving on and we look forward to it. As we seek to be obedient to the Great Commission and make disciples of the men and women God has led onto our path, we want them to go out from us as transformed disciple makers. And we know that God is in charge of their going. He has simply entrusted us with their equipping while they are with us. Our churches exist to know Jesus and make Him known. There is no better way to carry the gospel than to be sent out of a Christ-centered church as a military missionary funded by the U.S. government.

To be absolutely clear, God plants churches. We get to come alongside God to be faithful and obedient to do what His Word calls us to do. It is not really a strategy so much as it is an expectation of every Christian: make disciples. The difference is the disciples God has burdened our hearts for just happen to be military men, women and family members. They have needs, concerns, challenges and struggles like every other demographic where church planting is taking place across North America, and the rest of the world. They also have issues that are very unique to their situations, and require sensitivity and care that only the Holy Spirit and prayer can begin to reveal.

In spite of all the needs, concerns, challenges and struggles, God is faithful to build His Church. Our commitment to this belief shapes our practice. Therefore, we embrace the ever-changing face of our churches. We get excited at the prospect of who God might bring to us, according to His plan. We are encouraged to receive brothers and sisters who move in from an installation where another Pillar Church helped them grow in their faith. We also look forward to sending our best Bible teacher to another part of the world on a deployment or see our worship team cut in half due to a PCS move because we know it will result in the spread of the gospel to another coast. God's sovereign hand is sure and good, and when we believe that truth, we can rest in His providence.

8

MINISTERING TO "MILITARY BRATS" AND "DEPENDENT SPOUSES"

KELLI O'DAY
PILLAR CHURCH OF JACKSONVILLE, NORTH CAROLINA

ADDRESSING THE STEREOTYPES

The title of my chapter is intentional and specific. This is how we feel sometimes. This is how we are seen. Children of service members are called "brats" and will even introduce themselves as such. In response to the question, "Where are you from?" they will often answer, "I'm a military brat; I moved around a lot."

As spouses of service members, we often find our identity in the military's label for us – dependent spouse, as if our value and worth were likened to a leech who sits at home to suck the blood and treasure from the U.S. government.

However, these labels do not accurately reflect the great military spouses and children I know. The wives of service members (mostly Marines in my context) are some of the most capable, competent, confident, interdependent, loving and loyal women you could ever find. I know of many who personify the "Proverbs 31 Woman." She is an "excellent wife ... The heart of her husband trusts in her ... She does him good and not harm ... She rises while it is yet night and provides food for her household ... She dresses herself with strength and makes her arms strong ... Her lamp does not go out at night ... She opens her hand to the poor ... She is not afraid of snow for her household ... Strength and dignity are her clothing ... She opens her mouth with wisdom and the teaching of kindness is on her tongue" (Proverbs 31:10-26).

In addition, the children I know are energetic, resilient, fun-loving and out-going. They have moved; they have lost; they have been lonely; they have cried; they have hugged their dad and known that they would not see him for "a really long time." However, they have bounced back; they have laughed; they have been to new places; met new friends; explored new play-grounds; and reunited with their family after long separation. These children know that life is not easy, and many of them thrive and excel under the pressure.

These are the families I love, minister to and pray for. I did not come willingly[5], but I am thankful to God that I am here.

REAL CHALLENGES

The military lifestyle, however, is not without real and significant challenges for the families. It can be a lonely life – new house, new friends, husband/father gone, new city, new church and new responsibilities are all a way of life. I am from North Carolina – born and raised – and rarely left my mom's and dad's side growing up. The day after my wedding, however, I flew with my Marine to Fort Sill, Okla. After only four months of marriage we moved again, this time to Camp Lejeune, N.C. (still five and

---

[5] I was quite content as a Marine wife of 7-plus years when my husband told me of his plans to leave the Marine Corps and plant a church. "I don't want to be a pastor's wife!" my soul screamed.

one half hours from my parents). I unpacked our moving truck with a stranger as my husband prepared to get on a ship. The next few months he would be gone more than he was home (whatever "home" meant). Then, during our ninth month of marriage, he deployed – for six months. This was just the beginning. Ten years of active duty, five moves, at least three deployments and countless nights away training "in the field," or God only knows what else they do when they leave. It was hard. I was lonely. I now tell women, "It's okay to cry. This is hard."

It can be a confusing life. It often feels as though we have endless un-answered questions – "When are you leaving? When are you getting back? Where are you going? What will you be doing? Will you be able to be at _____ (fill in any special event)? When are we moving? Where are we going?

When we are together we are different people than we were when he departed. I have been here. He has been there. What did he see? Why is he different? What did he have to do? Why won't he talk to me, but will talk to his buddies? Have I changed too? What has changed? Will we ever be able to get back to "us?" What did "us" even look like?

It can quickly become an unbiblical life – even for strong Christians. Substance abuse (alcohol, prescription drugs, street drugs), adultery, gos-sip, slander, discontentment, bitterness and hopelessness are all too normal. What about God-honoring roles in the home? Husbands are to lead in the home, but who does it when he's not here? How does he resume that role when he returns? Isn't it easier to just keep the wife in leadership until this is all over? How long is that? Four years? Ten years? Twenty years? Thirty years?

GOSPEL SOLUTIONS

There is hope – the good news of Jesus Christ! I now see my role (as a former military spouse who knows the ropes and a pastor's wife who is to love the flock) as one who teaches truth and tangibly loves.

I constantly want to speak truth into the lives of these families. I want to teach and remind them that God is sovereign. He is sovereign, even in the hard times, even in the times of not-knowing, and even in the pain. I want to give them an eternal perspective. I want them to know that God is doing something in them and through them that may not be seen by them this week or this month. I want to show them that there are others who are struggling as much or more than they are. I want the older women (like more spiritually mature 20-somethings and above) to teach and encourage the younger women in a Titus 2:3-5 fashion.

In the inside of my prayer journal and the inside cover of my Bible I have verses that I am constantly reading with the ladies to remind them of these things.

> "But he said to me, 'My grace is sufficient for you, for my power is made perfect in weakness.' Therefore I will boast all the more gladly of my weaknesses, so that the power of Christ may rest upon me. For the sake of Christ, then, I am content with weaknesses, insults, hardships, persecutions, and calamities. For when I am weak, then I am strong."
>
> – 2 Corinthians 12:9-10

> "You keep him in perfect peace
> whose mind is stayed on you,
> because he trusts in you"
>
> – Isaiah 26:3

> "Come to me, all who labor and are heavy laden, and I will give you rest. Take my yoke upon you, and learn from me, for I am gentle and lowly in heart, and you will find rest for your souls. For my yoke is easy, and my burden is light."
>
> – Matthew 11:28-30

"And let us not grow weary of doing good, for in due season we will reap, if we do not give up. So then, as we have opportunity, let us do good to everyone, and especially to those who are of the household of faith."

– Galatians 6:9-10

CONCLUSION

These families have real challenges and trials, but the gospel is good news for their souls. I pray that we minister to their souls and love these precious families with the love of Christ.

9
THE SIGNIFICANCE
OF SACRIFICE

JOHNNY GRIFFITH, JR.
PILLAR CHURCH OF KANEOHE, HAWAII

The most often used phrase I hear when describing the network's ministry in my context is, "Oh you are really suffering for Jesus." You see, I am in the process of planting Pillar Church of Kaneohe, which is right outside of Marine Corps Hawaii. Yep, that's right, I'm in Hawaii. Now, before you skip to the next chapter thinking this guy knows nothing about sacrifice, please hear me out and understand what it took to get here.

I am a native Georgia boy with two great kids and a loving wife. I served six years in the Marine Corps, Semper Fi, and was medically retired. About eight years ago, I went from Marine to minister. I served in various leadership capacities, from youth pastor to senior pastor, but I always had a burden for the military. One evening I came across an article about the Praetorian Project and was blown away by what I read. I quickly shared the article with my wife and after praying, we knew that this was what we needed to be doing. Now, here is where the sacrifice began.

In the beginning, I did not sacrifice any possessions or even money. My first sacrifice was relationships. I had to resign from a church that I had committed almost four years of my life serving. In those four years I was not just part of a church that was experiencing revitalization, but was becoming part of the community, and in a lot of ways, becoming part of a family. It was hard to say goodbye to these people to whom I had fallen in love with, but this was not the greatest sacrifice that I would experience.

The greatest sacrifice was the sacrifice of certainty. I had become, in many ways, complacent in the security of being a pastor of an established church, but I was now starting something that was altogether new to me.

After resigning from the church, my family and 1 left Georgia and moved to Jacksonville, N.C., to begin an apprenticeship to become a church planter. We arrived in Jacksonville clinging on to the hope that we had six months' worth of support. Those six months flew by and I learned a lot. The first thing I learned is that as a church planter, and especially in this network, we are not certain about anything except God. I learned that my identity is not in my work, but in the work of Christ. Most importantly, I learned the reality of Paul's words written in Romans 5:1-5. I learned that through sacrifice, I could rejoice in God. I came to realize that through sacrifice came endurance, then character and then hope. All of this strengthened my faith, because every time I thought that there was no way, He showed me that there was. This was important, and in looking back, it was providential. God was only beginning to work.

Through my time as an apprentice and seeking where God wanted us, we felt Hawaii was the place. Not because of it's beauty, but because of it's people. While visiting, it was overwhelmingly apparent that there was a need for a gospel-centered church that would intentionally strive to reach the military. In realizing where God wanted my family and I, we knew the cost of moving and ministry would be astronomically high. Therefore, we began the hard work of asking people and churches to come alongside and partner with us in this ministry through both prayer and financial support.

Guess what my family heard the most? You guessed it, "Oh you are really going to suffer for Jesus." Well, we did. We sold everything we had except our vehicles, 12 medium size boxes of stuff and one suitcase of clothes for each of us. Now, let me paint the picture here. Both of our vehicles were paid for and were cheaper to transport than to replace. There were four of us, so we had to go through all of our individual possessions and get rid of everything that would not fit into twelve boxes. Each one of my children, ages 10 and 11, only had two boxes for their belongings, I had three boxes, and my wife had four boxes. Then, we each had a suitcase to put our clothes in. Each suitcase could only weigh 50 lbs. You should have seen the yard sale. We later arrived in Hawaii, but only with the uncertainty of where we would live, four suitcases, and twelve boxes and two cars on the way. We had seven days to find a home. But again, our greatest sacrifice is the sacrifice of certainty. By the providential hand of God, we found a place within five days and are stoked to be here.

Now, to be honest, I did not write this chapter with the goal of teaching you anything about sacrifice, even though I have learned much through my sacrifice. I figured that if you are reading this, you already know that as a disciple of Christ, we are to deny ourselves, pick up our crosses daily, and follow Him. I wrote this chapter to share my story, not that it is powerful or in any way worthy of anything, but to share what is real. In this network, we have all sacrificed for what we feel God has called us to do. Not just as church planters, but as parents, children and spouses. We have all given much, but our hope is in God, and in Him we find our identity and our purpose.

10
SAINTS AND SINNERS

TRACE MARTINEZ
PILLAR CHURCH OF OCEANSIDE, CALIFORNIA

One of the most unique features of military culture is the very small amount of people who have experienced it. Less than 1% of Americans are currently serving in the military with around 7% having served at some point in their lifetime. At first, this may seem like a severe disadvantage in trying to reach our military community, when in fact it creates opportunities for gospel advance. One of the primary ways a local church can impact the life of a service member is by serving as their family while they are away from home. In an authentic church family environment, people experience a kind of accountability that allows for the "one another" care we read about in the New Testament. It creates a sense of trust that opens doors for our fellow brothers and sisters in Christ to address some of the darker realities that come with life in the military.

There are plenty of obvious differences between military and civilian life. However, many of the things that the civilian community takes for granted in terms of moral or ethical living do not translate into military culture. Perhaps this stems from the segment of society that comprised a portion of our military not all that long ago. There was a time when the ranks were filled with men who had the choice between joining the military and going to jail. This is not meant to downplay their service in any way. But that alone created its own subculture within the military that has never truly gone away. Combine that with the fact that volunteering for service, with the knowledge that you may go to war and never come back, attracts a certain type of person. These factors, along with a few others outlined below, create an abnormal lifestyle that is very different from what the other 93% of Americans know and experience.

You're probably asking yourself, what's so different? For starters the military is a male dominated environment. For that reason, certain types of behavior are more tolerated than in other settings. For example, pornography is openly talked about and even celebrated in some circles. Crude jokes and language are also common place among military members. This may not actually come as a surprise, but what should be a surprise is the kind of behavior this can lead to. Sexual assault in the military is at an all-time high and is a product of the environment our men and women in uniform face every day. Adultery rates among military couples are so high that it is practically dismissed in many cases. It's almost as if it were excused because of the constant separation and other hardships they face. As a result, the divorce rate among military couples is incredibly high. Each week, the line for walk-in appointments to see a divorce attorney is out the door, and it doesn't show signs of slowing down.

There are other unique aspects of military life as well. Living in base housing is different. In what other environment do you live among the people with whom you work? You can't really ever get away from it. Another factor is the level of compensation for the amount of work performed. Our military members work long, hard hours and aren't paid especially well. This fact is compounded by people getting married very young, being away from home, and needing (desiring) to build a home for their family. That costs money – money that most of them don't have. The answer? Charge it!

And they do. The level of debt that many young service members carry is staggering. There is little done in the way of financial counseling until there is a problem. There are good resources made available by the military, but they are underutilized.

What in the world does all this have to do with church planting and reaching military members with the gospel? Quite frankly, you have to know what you're up against. As you were reading this snapshot of military culture, hopefully your mind began to formulate some ideas on ways to effectively minister to our service men and women. There are essentially four broad categories or features of military life that provide opportunity for gospel advance: home away from home (church as family), marriage, finances and sexual immorality. These are inroads for building relationships based on the needs of those in uniform that will lead to gospel conversations. If you have information that directly relates to a real need in their life, you have a way to transcend the boundaries that may exist between you and them.

Establishing a culture in your church that doesn't shy away from identifying and talking about these kinds of issues is the first step. Educating the members of your church with information about military culture is also necessary in reaching this section of society. Don't attempt to "be one of them" or pretend you know what it's like to serve in uniform (unless of course you have served). This has to be done in a way as not to alienate military members, rather to let them know you understand some of the challenges they face and you have a sincere desire to help. That help comes in the form of the love, grace and mercy of Jesus Christ. This can be a difficult truth to communicate if you can't overcome the boundaries that exist between you and them. As this chapter draws to a close, hopefully you have better insight into the unique culture within the military and have a few more ideas for gospel advance through these opportunities.

Made in the USA
Las Vegas, NV
15 October 2021